Big Mud Run

T0337124

Written by Zoë Clarke

Collins

Can you go on a mud run?

3

Get set and go!

They dash off!

Then they jog and zigzag.

hop

They hang on and kick.

They sink in the mud.

mud bank

They rush to win.

They are quick!

/qu/

14

/w/

 After reading

Letters and Sounds: Phase 3

Word count: 42

Focus phonemes: /j/ /w/ /z/ /qu/ /sh/ /th/ /ng/ /nk/

Common exception words: you, they, are, go, to, the

Curriculum links: Understanding the world: People and Communities

Early learning goals: Listening and attention: children listen attentively in a range of situations; Understanding: answer 'how' and 'why' questions about their experiences and in response to stories or events; Reading: read and understand simple sentences, use phonic knowledge to decode regular words and read them aloud accurately, read some common irregular words, demonstrate understanding when talking with others about what they have read

Developing fluency

- Your child may enjoy hearing you read the story.
- You could take turns to read a page. Model reading with lots of expression and encourage your child to do the same.

Phonic practice

- Look at pages 12–13 together. Ask your child:
  - Can you find a word that begins with the **w** phoneme? (*win*) Now sound out the word and blend the sounds together 'w-i-n' 'win'.
  - Can you find a word that begins with the **qu** phoneme? (*quick*) Now sound out the word and blend the sounds together 'qu-i-ck' 'quick'.
- Look at the 'I spy sounds' pages (14–15) together. How many words can your child point out that contain the **w** sound or the **qu** sound? (*winner, wet, quench, quick*)

Extending vocabulary

- Ask your child if they can tell you the opposite of each of the following words (opposites/antonyms):

  quick (*slow*) win (*lose*) go (*stop*)
- Can they think of any other pairs of antonyms?